AF228501

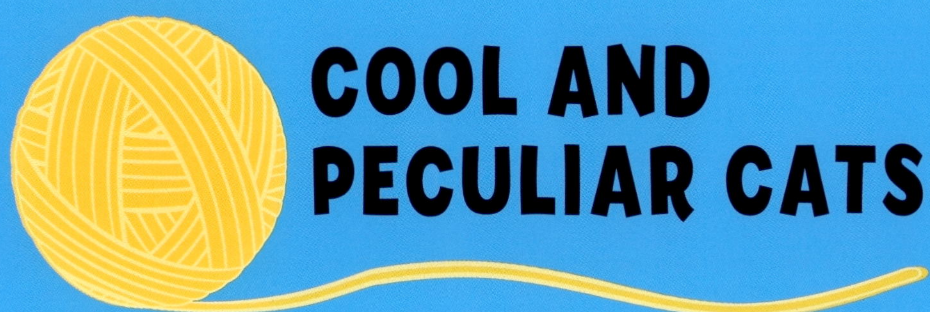

COOL AND PECULIAR CATS

Written by Eliza Jeffery

Illustrated by Marina Halak

First published in 2024 by Hungry Tomato Ltd
F15, Old Bakery Studios, Blewetts Wharf, Malpas Road, Truro, Cornwall,
TR1 1QH, UK.

A CIP catalog record for this book is available from the British Library.

ISBN 9781835690024

Manufactured in the USA

Discover more at
www.hungrytomato.com

CONTENTS

Words in **BOLD** can be found in the glossary.

THE WORLD OF CATS

Get ready to explore the wonderful world of cats! From the large Maine coon to the little Singapura, there are so many different types of curious cats to discover.

WHAT IS A SPECIES?

A species is a group of living things, like animals or plants, that share **unique** characteristics. For example, tigers and **domestic** cats are two different species. There are around 40 cat species in total, some of which can be separated into smaller groups called breeds.

WHAT IS A BREED?

A breed is a small group of animals within a species that all share the same (or very similar) appearance and characteristics, making them easy to identify. There are lots of different breeds, and they can vary wildly in size, shape, hairiness, and personality.

Not all cats belong to a specific breed. Some cats are a mixture of lots of different breeds. They can make fantastic and unique pets, and can often be found looking for a loving home at rescue or **rehoming shelters**.

WHERE DO CATS COME FROM?

All cats are **descendants** of the African wildcat, a species believed to have appeared 12 million years ago! This cat is still around today, alongside many other types of wild cat. There are plenty of new species that have been domesticated by humans too – these are the types of cats that we keep as pets!

GETTING A CAT?

Maybe you already have a cat in your family, or maybe you'd like to in the future. Owning a cat can be fun and rewarding, but it's also a big responsibility. Some cats need a lot of grooming, care and attention. Before buying or adopting a cat, you should always carefully research their breed and think about whether you are able to give them everything they need to be happy.

EXERCISE AND PLAY

When it comes to taking care of a cat, there is a lot to consider! Some cats need a lot more looking after than others. Here are a few things to think about when you're looking into what your cat needs to be happy and healthy.

PLAYTIME

Regardless of whether your cat lives indoors or is allowed to explore the world outside, exercise is important for keeping your cat happy. And the best way for your pet to exercise is through play!

You might want to get involved with playtime, too! This is the perfect way to bond with your cat and make sure it is staying active. Exercise and play are very important in keeping your cat happy, as well as healthy!

A ball of string will keep a cat entertained for ages!

EVERYDAY EXERCISE

Although different cats require slightly different levels of fitness, it is recommended that 30 minutes a day of exercise is a good amount of time for a cat to stay healthy. Unlike dogs, cats don't need long and energetic walks.

Cats that are allowed outdoors will spend lots of their time on the move, but short play sessions at home throughout the day are a great way to keep them happy too. Old cats and cats with health problems will only need short bursts of exercise.

Indoor cats need plenty of exercise, too!

WALKING AN INDOOR CAT

If you have an indoor cat (page 24), you can make sure they stay healthy and get enough exercise by walking them on a lead too. It may take your cat some getting used to, but it is a great opportunity for your indoor cat to explore, as well as keep fit.

COOL CAT FEATURES

Explore the unique features that make cats such fascinating creatures! From their sharp claws to their clever tails, uncover the impressive adaptations that help cats thrive in their **environments**.

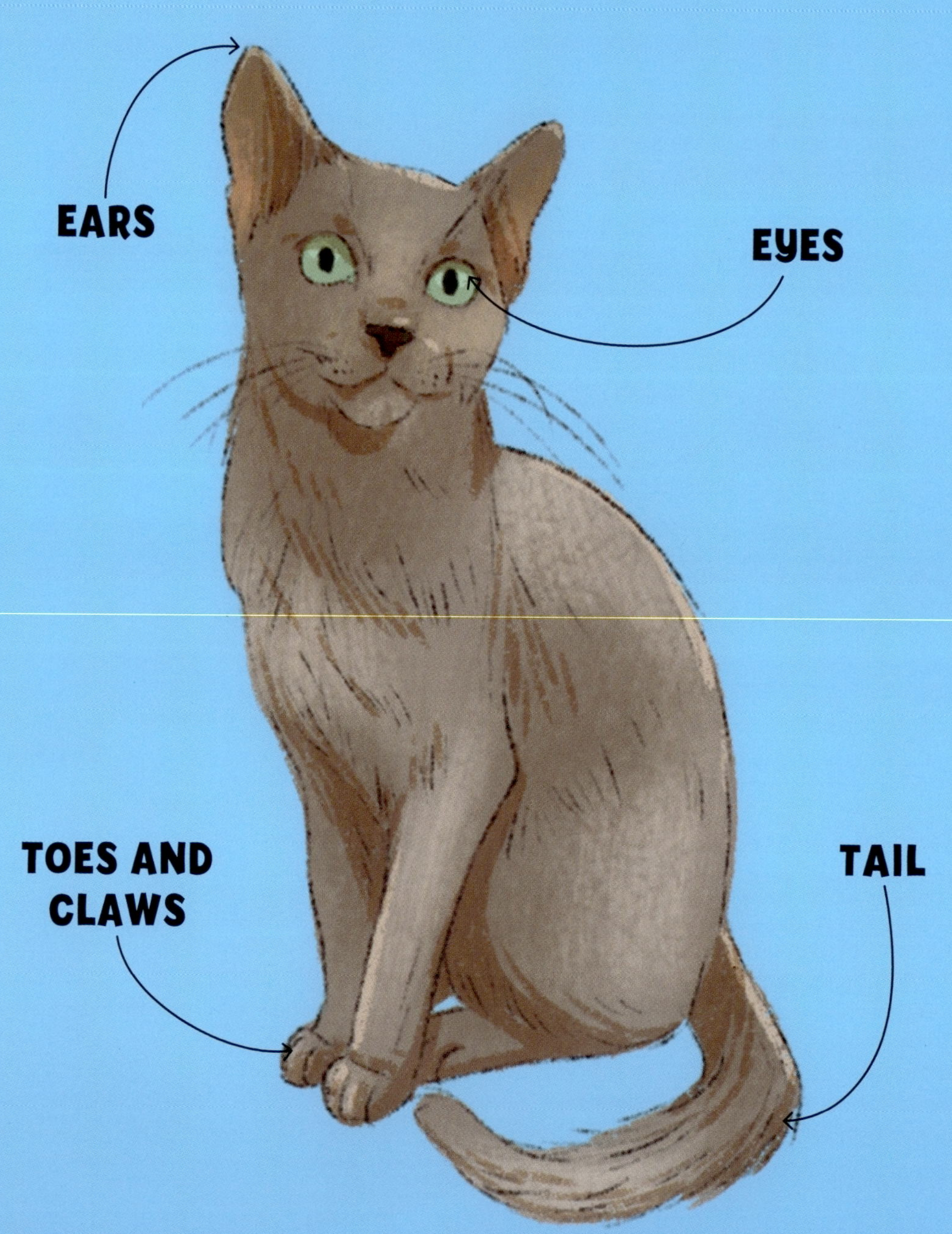

EARS

Cats are able to move each ear independently! This means one ear can be pointing out one way, listening for sounds, while the other can be pointing in the opposite direction.

EYES

Cats have excellent eyesight. Cats can see eight times better than humans can in the dark! They also have an extra eyelid on each eye that protects them from harm, which can't usually be seen.

TOES AND CLAWS

Cats are digitigrade, which means they can walk on their toes! Each toe has a curved claw, which can retract back into the skin.

TAIL

Cats use their tails to help them balance. They have lots of muscles in their tails, which help them move easily and in lots of different ways. Cats also use their tails to show how they are feeling.

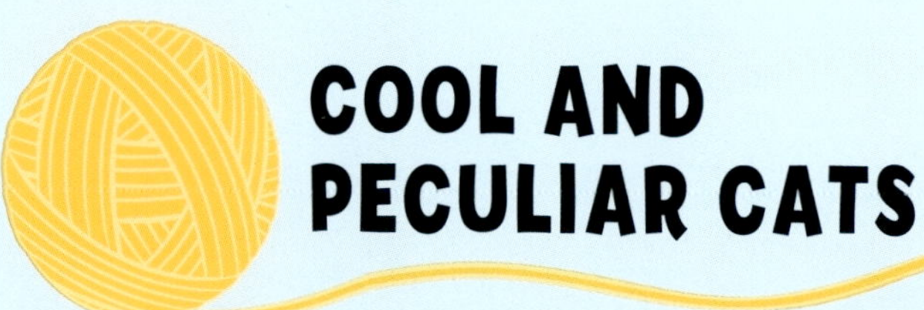

COOL AND PECULIAR CATS

Ever wondered how big the biggest cat really is?
Or what a cat with no tail might look like? How about a
cat with extremely short legs?

From cats with curly coats to felines without a matching
pair of eyes, these quirky and charming characteristics
make these one-of-a-kind cats stand out from the crowd.
Let's check out the cats with cool and peculiar features!

Maine Coon

The Maine coon is the largest domestic cat breed in the world. This impressive feline is celebrated as the native cat of America. They have a thick, waterproof coat that thickens in colder months and sheds in warmer months. They can be as big as a medium-sized dog!

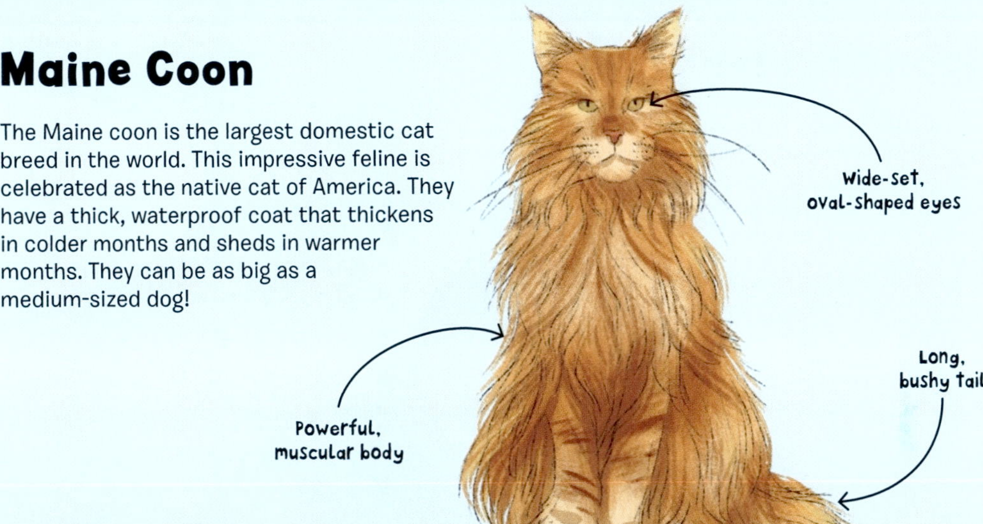

ORIGIN: USA

COAT: Silky and smooth

PERSONALITY: Friendly and gentle

GROOMING

AFFECTION

PLAYFULNESS

Singapura

The Singapura is the smallest cat breed in the world. Despite being small in size, these energetic felines make up for it with their big personalities! They can be very mischievous, and love to explore the world around them.

ORIGIN: United Kingdom

COAT: Short and smooth

PERSONALITY: Intelligent and curious

GROOMING    

AFFECTION

PLAYFULNESS

American Wirehair

The American wirehair is best known for its unusual **wiry** coat! The **crimped** fur curls round on itself, making its coat bristly and rough to touch. These cats enjoy playing with their owners but much prefer a quieter indoor space.

ORIGIN: USA	**GROOMING**
COAT: Wiry and coarse	**AFFECTION**
PERSONALITY: Friendly and active	**PLAYFULNESS**

Ural Rex

The Ural Rex has a curly coat too! This is a popular breed for families, due to its patient and playful nature. Gentle, but confident, the Ural Rex will make friends with anybody that it can, including other household pets (even dogs!).

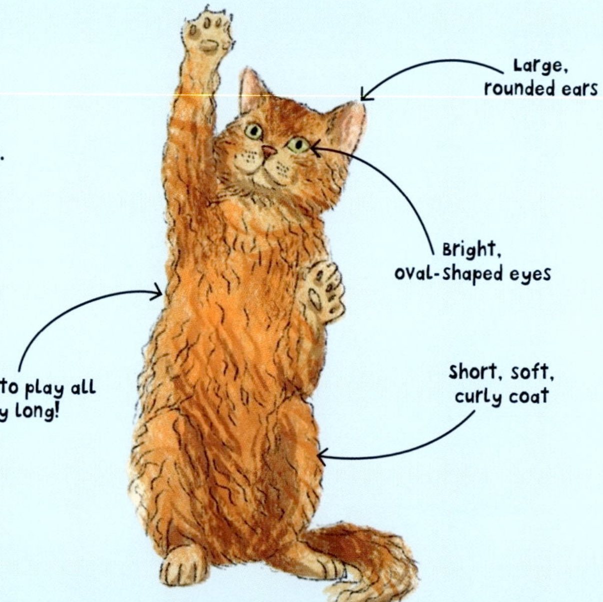

ORIGIN: Russia	**GROOMING**
COAT: Long and wavy	**AFFECTION**
PERSONALITY: Quiet but friendly	**PLAYFULNESS**

Sphynx

Sphynx are most well-known for having no fur at all! These hairless felines were named because of how similar they looked to the Egyptian **monument** of the Sphinx. Though their appearance is not appealing to everybody, these cats are very loving and friendly.

ORIGIN: Canada

COAT: None!

PERSONALITY: Energetic and intelligent

GROOMING

AFFECTION

PLAYFULNESS

Lykoi

Because of its unusual coat, the Lykoi is often described as looking like a werewolf! This active feline is partially hairless, with thin fur unevenly covering its body. They may look like **feral** creatures, but these cats make excellent, playful pets.

ORIGIN: USA

COAT: Uneven and soft

PERSONALITY: Outgoing and vocal

GROOMING

AFFECTION

PLAYFULNESS

Khao Manee

Khao Manees can have blue, yellow or green eyes and sometimes they don't have a matching pair! They are very talkative and will purr or chirp loudly when they are happy. These fascinating felines are loyal to their owners and do not like to be away from them for too long!

ORIGIN: Thailand

COAT: Short and smooth

PERSONALITY: Active and people-loving

GROOMING

AFFECTION

PLAYFULNESS

Ojos Azules

Ojos Azules is considered an extremely rare breed. But the distinctive feature that makes this feline stand out is its unusually bright blue eyes! Its breed name even means 'blue eyes' in Spanish.

ORIGIN: USA

COAT: Short and fine

PERSONALITY: Friendly and gentle

GROOMING

AFFECTION

PLAYFULNESS

Russian Blue

Russian blue cats are easy to spot, as they have beautiful, bluish coats and piercing, green eyes. It takes roughly four months for these felines to develop these bright eyes, sometimes starting off as shades of amber or yellow.

ORIGIN: Russia

COAT: Thick and dense

PERSONALITY: Calm and shy

GROOMING

AFFECTION

PLAYFULNESS

Siamese

One of the most well-known cat breeds in the world is the Siamese. These elegant felines need lots of playtime, especially outdoors. As well as enjoying calm environments, these curious cats love to climb and explore!

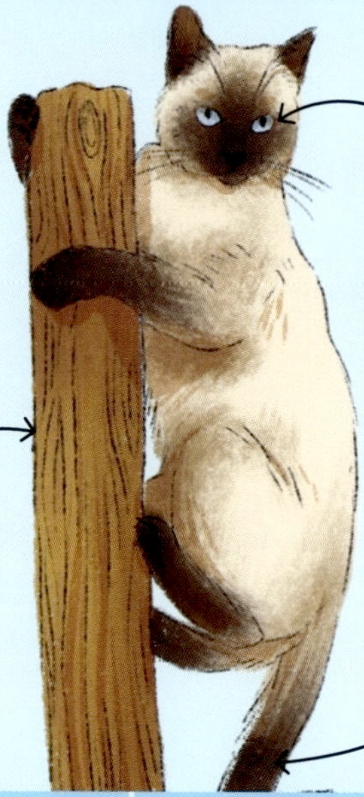

ORIGIN: Thailand

COAT: Fine and short

PERSONALITY: Sociable and athletic

GROOMING				
AFFECTION				
PLAYFULNESS				

Munchkin

Munchkins have extremely short legs! Despite their small size, these active felines love to play high-energy games with their owners and can run very fast. This unique breed can be either long-haired or short-haired.

ORIGIN: USA

COAT: Smooth and thick

PERSONALITY: Loyal and energetic

GROOMING				
AFFECTION				
PLAYFULNESS				

Chausie

The Chausie was originally believed to have developed from a mix of wildcat and domestic cat, giving it its untamed appearance. This striking feline requires lots of company and attention from its owners, and is known to get along well with dogs!

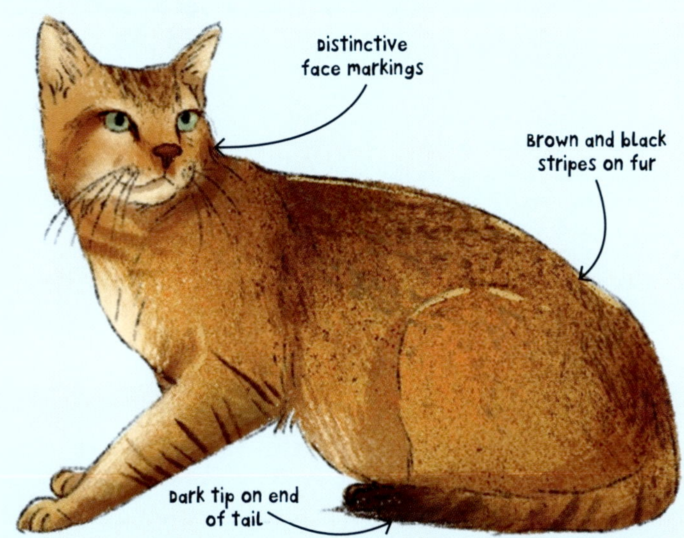

ORIGIN: USA

COAT: Short and silky

PERSONALITY: Active and curious

GROOMING

AFFECTION

PLAYFULNESS

Egyptian Mau

The Egyptian Mau is one of the only domesticated cats that has a naturally spotted coat. This majestic breed dates back to ancient Egypt, and can be seen in many **tomb** paintings from the time. Although they can be very loving toward their owners, they're very shy and cautious around anybody else!

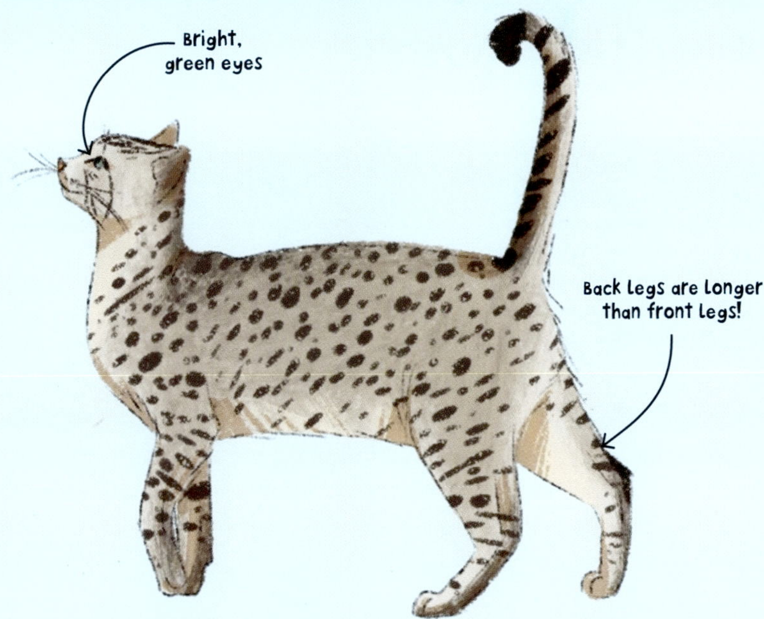

ORIGIN: Egypt

COAT: Short and dense

PERSONALITY: Friendly and loyal

GROOMING

AFFECTION

PLAYFULNESS

Japanese Bobtail

The Japanese bobtail is easy to spot because of its small, round tail that looks just like the tail of a rabbit. This breed originated in Japan and is believed to bring good luck. This sweet feline would be happy playing with its owners all day long!

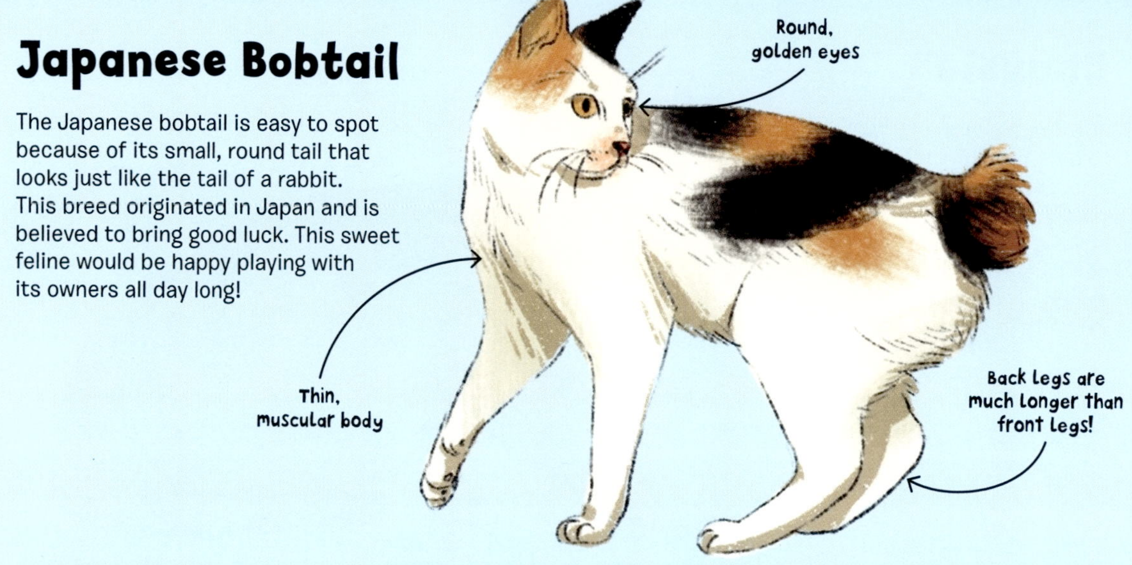

ORIGIN: Japan

COAT: Silky and soft

PERSONALITY: Intelligent and outgoing

GROOMING

AFFECTION

PLAYFULNESS

American Ringtail

Like its name suggests, the American ringtail is easily spotted by its tail that is twisted into the shape of a ring. This unique-looking feline is the only cat breed to have a tail like this. They are curious cats, with a particular love for climbing.

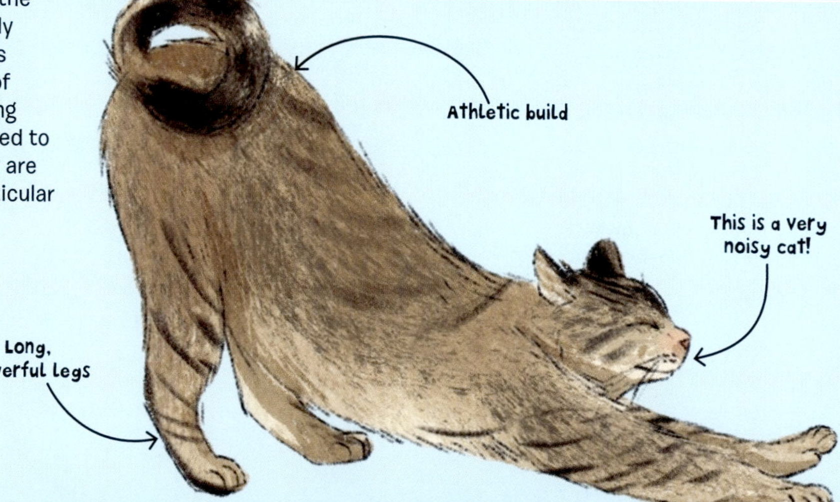

ORIGIN: USA

COAT: Silky and soft

PERSONALITY: Active and vocal

GROOMING 

AFFECTION 

PLAYFULNESS 

Pixiebob

The Pixiebob gets its name from its extremely short tail. Despite looking like its wildcat relative, the bobcat, this feline is known for its sweet, gentle nature and love of being around people. They are also described as having dog-like personalities because they enjoy playing in water!

ORIGIN: USA	**GROOMING** 🐾🐾🐾🐾🐾
COAT: Woolly and dense	**AFFECTION** 🐾🐾🐾🐾🐾
PERSONALITY: Intelligent and sociable	**PLAYFULNESS** 🐾🐾🐾🐾🐾

Manx

Manx cats have no tail at all! Instead, the end of their small bodies have a short stump where the tail should be. This unusual breed is popular with cat owners for its unique appearance and sweet nature. They are very curious cats, playing with anything they find!

ORIGIN: United Kingdom	**GROOMING** 
COAT: Thick and dense	**AFFECTION** 
PERSONALITY: Gentle and calm	**PLAYFULNESS** 

Scottish Fold

Scottish folds are best known for having large, golden eyes and folded over ears! Their unique ears bend forward and lay flat against their head. These cats are known for being very loyal creatures, and love quality time with their owners.

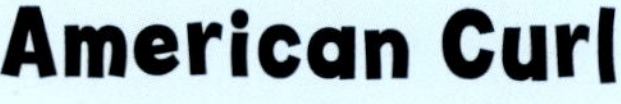

ORIGIN: Scotland

COAT: Short and dense

PERSONALITY: Quiet and friendly

GROOMING

AFFECTION

PLAYFULNESS

American Curl

Similar to the Highlander (page 21), the American curl, as its name suggests, has ears that curl far back on the top of its head. Sociable and nosy, American curls love to be involved in their owners' lives, 'helping' them as much as possible!

ORIGIN: USA

COAT: Soft and silky

PERSONALITY: Loving and engaging

GROOMING

AFFECTION

PLAYFULNESS

Highlander

The Highlander is a fairly new breed of cat and is best known for ears that bend backward. These energetic cats are always in the mood to play! They are loyal to their owners, and can be either short-haired or long-haired.

FUN CAT FACTS

What else is there to know about the wonderful world of cats? Let's uncover more interesting facts about these fascinating felines.

AFFECTIONATE CATS

Cats lick their owners to show they care! A cat associates licking with caring as it is something they learn from their mothers, who lick their kittens from birth. As they grow, kittens carry on sharing the love with those around them, whether they are cats or humans!

Your cat's tongue may be rough, but its a sign of love!

AND JUMP!

Cats of all kinds are known for their agility. On average, a cat can jump up to six times their height in one jump! How impressive is that?

LANDING FEET FIRST

As well as jumping up high, cats are impressive when they land back down too! All cats are born with the "righting reflex", a system which allows them to move in mid-air so they land paws first.

WHISKERS ALL OVER

Cats don't just have whiskers on their face! All cats have carpal whiskers too, which are special whiskers found on their front legs, just above their paws. The carpal whiskers help cats climb trees, as well as help them navigate their environment.

INDOOR OR OUTDOOR CATS

An important decision to make when getting a feline friend is whether they will be an indoor or outdoor cat. While both options have their benefits and risks, it's important to think about what's best for your own cat's safety, health, and overall happiness.

INDOOR CATS

Some cats prefer not go outside on their own, but may explore the outside world with their owner. There are positives to keeping your cat indoors, such as protecting them from outdoor dangers, like cars and predators.

However, indoor cats may sometimes feel restless, so they need plenty of toys and activities to keep them entertained. They may also become more nervous compared to outdoor cats, who are used to the sights and sounds of the outside world.

It's important for indoor cats to have plenty of physical exercise, attention, and play to keep them happy and healthy.

American wirehair cats are indoor cats as they prefer the comfort of their home.

OUTDOOR CATS

Outdoor cats are cats that are allowed to explore the outside world without their owner. Going outdoors can be enjoyable for your cat as it gives them the freedom and space to explore, as well as to hunt.

However, outdoor cats face risks such as the possibility of injury from fights with other animals or getting sick from **diseases**. **Parasites** like fleas and ticks are something that owners will have to regularly check their cat's fur for.

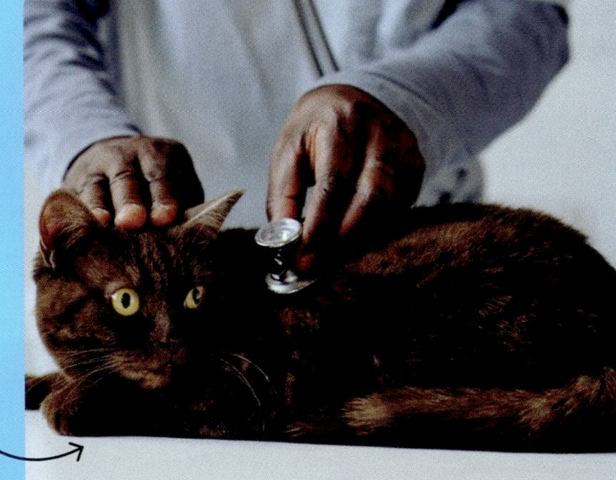

Outdoor cats sometimes bring **rodents** they've hunted and caught back to the house! Although we might not be too happy about it, cats often bring back their **prey** as a gift for their owners!

NAME THAT CAT

Can you work out which cat each of these pictures are a part of? Clues have been provided for you based on facts in this book.

CLUE: These cats are believed to be a mix of wildcat and domestic cat.

CLUE: These cats look a bit like werewolves due to their unusual, partially hairless coat.

CLUE: These cats are the largest domestic breed in the world!

CLUE: These cats are named after their bright blue eyes!

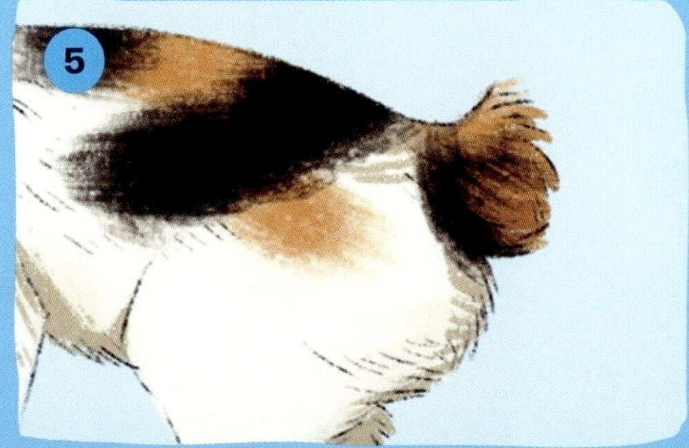

CLUE: These cats are easy to spot due to their small, round tail that looks like the tail of a rabbit.

CLUE: These cats are known for having large, golden eyes and folded over ears that lay flat against their heads.

CLUE: These cats have a tail that is twisted into the shape of a ring.

CLUE: These cats have extremely short legs.

CLUE: These cats are the smallest cat breed in the world!

CLUE: These cats are well-known for having no fur at all! They look similar to the Egyptian monument of the Sphinx.

Answers can be found on page 32.

WHAT'S THAT CAT?

Now that you have read all about these curious cats, how good are you at identifying them? There are 20 different cats to figure out. Use the information in the book to help you.

1

What am I?
A. Maine Coon
B. Singapura
C. Chausie

2

What am I?
A. Khao Manee
B. Singapura
C. Munchkin

3

What am I?
A. Manx
B. American Curl
C. Ojos Azules

4

What am I?
A. Siamese
B. Scottish Fold
C. Ural Rex

5

What am I?
A. Sphynx
B. Highlander
C. Manx

6

What am I?
A. Russian Blue
B. Sphynx
C. Siamese

7

What am I?
A. Lykoi
B. Japanese Bobtail
C. Munchkin

8

What am I?
A. Egyptain Mau
B. Ojos Azules
C. Munchkin

9

What am I?
A. Ural Rex
B. Khao Manee
C. Russian Blue

10

What am I?
A. American Ringtail
B. Egyptian Mau
C. Pixiebob

Answers can be found on page 32.

What am I?
A. Chausie
B. American Wirehair
C. Manx

What am I?
A. Highlander
B. American Curl
C. Russian Blue

What am I?
A. Siamese
B. Japanese Bobtail
C. Scottish Fold

What am I?
A. Ojos Azules
B. Ural Rex
C. American Ringtail

What am I?
A. Lykoi
B. American Wirehair
C. Highlander

What am I?
A. Sphynx
B. Pixiebob
C. Scottish Fold

What am I?
A. Scottish Fold
B. Lykoi
C. Khao Manee

What am I?
A. Maine Coon
B. Pixiebob
C. Singapura

What am I?
A. American Wirehair
B. Maine Coon
C. Egyptian Mau

What am I?
A. American Curl
B. Chausie
C. Siamese

GLOSSARY

Crimped - fur that has small ridges or folds in it.

Descendants – people or animals that are related to an individual or group who lived in the past. For example, you are a descendant of your parents and grandparents.

Diseases - conditions that cause part of a living thing to no longer work properly.

Domestic - an animal that has been tamed or trained to live or work with humans.

Environments - another word for surroundings.

Feral - wild, not domestic (see above).

Monument - a statue or building made in memory of a person or event.

Parasites - tiny creatures that live on or inside other living things, like animals or plants.

Prey - animals that are hunted and killed for food.

Rehoming shelter - a place where cats (or other animals) who were lost, stray or given up by their owners are looked after until they can be adopted into a new home.

Retract - to pull something back or make it go back inside.

Rodents - small mammals with sharp front teeth, such as mice or squirrels.

Slender - something that is thin and narrow.

Tomb - a large, underground space for burying and remembering the dead.

Unique - something that stands out and is completely different from everything else.

Wiry - a type of coat that is rough, thick and bristly.

INDEX

NAME THAT CAT ANSWERS

1 - Chausie
2 - Lykoi
3 - Maine Coon
4 - Ojos Azules

5 - Japanese Bobtail
6 - Scottish Fold
7 - American Ringtail
8 - Munchkin

9 - Singapura
10 - Sphynx

WHAT'S THAT CAT ANSWERS

1 - A. Maine Coon
2 - B. Singapura
3 - A. Manx
4 - C. Ural Rex
5 - A. Sphynx
6 - C. Siamese
7 - C. Munchkin

8 - B. Ojos Azules
9 - B. Khao Manee
10 - B. Egyptian Mau
11 - A. Chausie
12 - C. Russian Blue
13 - B. Japanese Bobtail
14 - C. American Ringtail

15 - C. Highlander
16 - C. Scottish Fold
17 - B. Lykoi
18 - B. Pixiebob
19 - A. American Wirehair
20 - A. American Curl

ABOUT THE AUTHOR

Eliza Jeffery is a children's book author based in Falmouth. She is passionate about helping children explore and enjoy the big world around them. She loves exploring Cornwall, and can often be found reading a book and eating a bowl of mussels by the sea!

ABOUT THE ILLUSTRATOR

Marina Halak is a talented illustrator of children's books from Ukraine. Her stunning illustrations are inspired by her own childhood, children, nature, magical moments and fairy tales. Marina is also the illustrator behind the series, *Dogs*.